# STRANGE
## BUT TRUE STORIES

------ **BOOK 2** ------

Bob Lazar, the UFO Guy
The Mothman Mystery
Mischievous Spirits
*...and More!*

Janet Lorimer

SADDLEBACK
EDUCATIONAL PUBLISHING

# STRANGE BUT TRUE STORIES

## BOOK 1

The Presidential Ghost
Mystery Spots on Earth
UFO or Weather
Balloon?

## BOOK 2

Bob Lazar, the UFO Guy
The Mothman Mystery
Mischievous Spirits

## BOOK 3

Phantom Ships
The Jersey Devil
Living Dinosaurs?

## BOOK 4

Skulls of Doom
Winchester Mystery House
What Lurks Beneath the Waves?

## BOOK 5

King Tut's Curse
Amazing Athletic Feats
Monster or Myth?

*...and More!*

SADDLEBACK
EDUCATIONAL PUBLISHING
www.sdlback.com

ISBN-13: 978-1-61651-766-3
ISBN-10: 1-61651-766-2
eBook: 978-1-61247-297-3

Printed in Malaysia

20 19 18 17 16   6 7 8 9 10

# CONTENTS

# STRANGE BUT TRUE STORIES

## LIZZIE BORDEN—
## DID SHE OR DIDN'T SHE?

*Lizzie Borden took an axe*
*And gave her mother forty whacks.*
*When she saw what she had done*
*She gave her father forty-one.*

(Anonymous)

It happened on August 4, 1892, in Fall River, Massachusetts. It was a warm summer's morning, a little after 11:00 A.M.

Lizzie Borden called out to the family maid, Bridget Sullivan, telling her to come quickly. Then Lizzie showed the maid a gruesome scene. Lizzie's father, Andrew Borden, was lying dead on the sofa in the downstairs parlor. The man had been brutally murdered.

Abby, Lizzie's stepmother, was later found dead in an upstairs bedroom. She and her husband had been hacked to death with either a hatchet or an axe.

Contrary to the legend, Abby had died from 18—not 40—blows to the head, and Andrew died from 11 blows.

After a one-week investigation, the police arrested Lizzie. She was kept in jail for almost a year before her trial began. The trial lasted only two weeks—but it was a coast-to-coast sensation. More than 40 newspapers from across the country sent reporters to cover the story. On a local playground, school children began to sing, *"Lizzie Borden took an axe . . . ."*

The evidence against 32-year-old Lizzie was largely circumstantial. When the police arrived at the Borden home, Lizzie had no bloodstains on her. And the exact weapon was never found.

Lizzie claimed she'd been in the barn for part of the morning. A witness came forward to state that he had seen a woman emerging from the barn. Another witness claimed to have seen a wild-eyed man fleeing from the house. But were the witnesses believable?

The prosecution, however, insisted that there was good reason to suspect Lizzie. At the time of the murders, the maid was outdoors washing windows. Lizzie's older sister was out of town, and a houseguest was out visiting relatives. At the time of her stepmother's death, Lizzie had been the only person in the house.

And Lizzie had a motive! Her father was one of the richest men in Fall River—but he was tight-fisted. No matter how Lizzie begged, he refused to move the family to a better neighborhood. And Lizzie desperately wanted to live on The Hill. There, she hoped to become part of Fall River "society."

Lizzie hated her stepmother, Abby. Did she want to kill her father and stepmother so she would inherit their money? Then a friend testified about what she saw three days after the murders. She watched as Lizzie burned a dress in the kitchen fire! Lizzie claimed it was an old dress stained with paint. But was it really paint—or was it blood?

The problem for the jurors was this: Abby Borden was killed at 9:30 in the morning. Andrew Borden died an hour and a half later. If Lizzie committed the murders, how did she clean herself up after Andrew's death? After all, she'd called to the maid shortly after 11:00. That was just minutes after Andrew had been murdered.

But how could an outsider have committed the murders? Where had he or she hidden for the hour and a half between the killings?

In the end, the all-male jury acquitted Lizzie. They simply could not believe that a refined young woman who taught Sunday school could commit such horrible crimes.

After the trial, Lizzie and her sister bought a huge house on The Hill. Sadly, the townspeople didn't welcome Lizzie into society. Even though she had been found not guilty, many people believed that she was.

Today, the Borden house at 92 Second Street is a bed and breakfast inn. Guests can spend the night in the room where—now more than 100 years ago—Lizzie's stepmother was slaughtered. They can sit on a replica of the sofa where Andrew Borden was hacked to death. They can also enjoy the same breakfast that the maid served to the Bordens so long ago. By all accounts, the rooms are booked for months in advance!

What's your opinion? Did Lizzie get away with murder? Your guess is as good as anyone else's!

## THE BEAST OF GEVAUDAN

People in France have a saying: "When twigs crack, don't whistle!" That means you shouldn't make a sound if you're alone in the woods and you hear twigs snapping. Something might be following you!

Perhaps this saying caught on because of the Beast of Gevaudan. It has been said that the Beast killed at least 100 people. Other sources say twice as many. No one will ever know the exact number.

The terror began in 1764. A young woman was out herding her cows in the French countryside. Then, suddenly, she was attacked by a huge beast! Luckily, the cows fended off the creature with their horns. The young woman escaped with only minor wounds.

Later she told the people in her village that the Beast looked something like a wolf. But no one had ever seen a wolf like this one! It was about the size of a cow. It had a wide chest, a huge head and neck, and short straight ears. Its nose was like a greyhound's, and its fangs were about an inch and a half long. A black stripe ran down its back from its head to the tip of its long, thin tail. But the most amazing thing about it, she added, was that it could leap as far as 30 feet at a time!

In the following months the beast continued to attack women and children. It also attacked lone men who were taking their livestock to pasture. Many of these people were torn apart, eaten, or carried off. Oddly enough, the Beast always attacked during the day.

In October, two hunters shot at the Beast. To their amazement, it fell down, but got up again. It fell again after a second shot, but it got up and ran unsteadily toward the woods. The hunters shot a third time. Once more the Beast fell, stood up, and ran.

The hunters were certain they'd soon find the Beast dead. Instead, over the next few days, the Beast furiously attacked even more people. Was the monster trying to get even for the wounds it suffered?

In November, a military man, Captain Duhamel, organized another hunt. He and his soldiers went after the Beast, setting trap after trap. But each time the Beast stepped in a snare, it somehow managed to escape.

Now a huge reward was offered. Hunters from all over France arrived. For months they hunted the Beast—with no luck! Meanwhile, the Beast continued its attacks right under the hunters' noses.

By now, word of the Beast had reached the King of France. King Louis XV sent a famous hunter, Monsieur Denneval, to the district. Supposedly, Denneval had killed 1,200 wolves.

In February 1765, Denneval started to track the Beast with his bloodhounds. But he had no luck either.

Then, in April, a nobleman spotted the Beast near his home. It was stalking a shepherd. The noblemen and his two brothers ambushed the creature. Though they shot at it, it managed to escape into the woods. But it left a lot of blood behind, so they knew they'd hit it. Had it limped away to die? They thought so.

Villagers turned out to celebrate the death of the Beast. In the middle of the celebration, however, a rider galloped into the village square. He announced that *he* had just killed the Beast.

The local people were enraged. They grabbed pitchforks, long poles, and bayonets—whatever they had at hand. Dogs were put onto the fresh scent and set off to find the Beast. But once more, the Beast was nowhere to be found.

The King was furious. His greatest hunter—Denneval—had given up. Now rumors were spreading that the Beast had to be a werewolf.

Antoine de Beauterne was the king's

official problem-solver. For three months he analyzed the situation. He studied the area and drew maps. He checked the routes taken by the Beast. Finally, in September, he organized a new hunt.

When hunters surrounded a ravine in the woods, the dogs suddenly began to bark wildly. The Beast, hiding in the ravine, was forced into the open. When it looked for a way to escape, De Beauterne shot it and it fell.

Then, to everyone's horror, the Beast got up. It was shot again, but, amazingly, it found a way through the circle of men! It ran into a nearby pasture and fell again. But this time the Beast did not move. At long last it really was dead!

When the hunters examined the Beast, they were amazed at its size. It was six feet long from its nose to the tip of its tail, and it weighed 143 pounds. Some time later its hide was stuffed. Then it was taken to the king, who put it into the Museum of Natural History.

It seemed that the terror of the local French people was over. Or was it?

For two more months, the killings went on! The king was frantic. He wouldn't allow anyone to speak of the problem. That winter was a nightmare for the local people. Not only was the Beast—or perhaps even a second Beast—attacking them, but they couldn't ask for help! The following year, 1766, the attacks continued. To this day no one knows how many people were killed, because no records were kept. Families weren't allowed to report that the Beast had slaughtered their loved ones.

Finally, in June 1767, another hunt was organized. One man, Jean Chastel, had three cartridges blessed for the occasion. He joined the hunt, placing himself in the same ravine where the first Beast had been trapped and killed.

While he patiently waited for the Beast to appear, he read his prayer book.

Then one day the Beast showed its

face. Trying to get away from the dogs, it ran out in front of Chastel. Chastel closed his prayer book, raised his gun, and fired. When the Beast fell, Chastel supposedly said, "You will kill no more!"

The Beast was dead. Again.

It is said that no grass will grow on the spot where the Beast fell.

And so . . . just what *was* the Beast of Gevaudan?

## EVP—IS THIS HOW THE DEAD TALK TO US?

People have been trying to talk to the dead for centuries. But can the dead ever talk back to us? Perhaps so, through Electronic Voice Phenomenon—EVP.

In 1959, a Swedish scientist named Friedrich Jurgenson went out into the countryside to make a tape of bird songs. When he played the tape back, he heard a man's deep voice speaking in a strange language. He seemed to be talking about nocturnal bird songs.

At first Jurgenson suspected he'd accidentally picked up a radio broadcast. He made more tapings, and while he was taping, he didn't hear any voices. But when he played the tape back, he heard many voices that seemed to convey personal information to him. He identified one voice as that of his dead mother.

Finally, he concluded that all the voices on the tape must have come from beyond the grave.

Jurgenson continued to experiment with EVP. In 1964, he published a book on the topic, *Voices From the Universe*.

When he read Jurgenson's book, a Latvian psychologist named Konstantin Raudive became interested in EVP. The two men met in 1965. Raudive recorded more than 100,000 voices speaking on tape. These recordings were of men, women, and children speaking in different languages. Today, electronic voices are also known as "Raudive voices."

In 1972, an English psychologist decided to try taping the voices of the dead. Speaking into the tape's microphone, he asked, "Can anyone hear me?" and "Would anyone like to speak to me?"

To his amazement, he got an answer. When he played back the tape, he heard the word "*Yes*" faintly pronounced in a hiss and rush of sound.

In 1986, a Swiss electronics engineer went further. He received pictures of the dead on a television screen. The device he used was called a "vidicom." It was a special TV that was switched on but not connected to an aerial. He positioned a video camera in front of the TV to videotape images on the screen.

Today, people all around the world continue to experiment with EVP. As new electronic devices become more sophisticated, more people say they're able to record the voices of the dead.

EVP has its critics, of course. Some say that researchers are accidentally picking up random radio broadcasts. Others claim that the voices heard on the tapes are just figments of the imagination. Until we can scientifically prove that the dead can actually talk to us, the controversy is sure to continue.

## THE ANTIKYTHERA MECHANISM— AN ANCIENT COMPUTER?

We people of the 21st century think of ourselves as light years ahead of previous civilizations. Look at our great technology! And think of the wonderful things we can do with computers. Too bad ancient people didn't have what we have.

*Or did they?*

In 1900, sponge divers found the remains of a Greek ship off the coast of an island near Crete. The divers brought up beautiful statues and bronze relics. None of the items seemed unusual until 1902. Then scientists noticed what looked like a *gear* in a small bronze relic. They named the artifact the *Antikythera Mechanism* after the island where it was found.

But wait a minute! How could there be cogwheels in an artifact more than 2,000 years old?

In 1951, Dr. Price, a British scientist, discovered complex gears in the device. Price continued to study the mechanism until 1971. Then the Greek Atomic Energy Commission X-rayed the device. When the photo showed how the gears meshed together, Price was astounded. It appeared that the ancient object had been part of a simple mechanical computer! Dr. Price guessed that this computer could display the position of the sun and moon on any given day.

As the study continued, scientists made working models of the mechanism. Sure enough, in the year 2002, one model accurately calculated the movements of the sun, the moon, and the planets.

Dr. Price was thrilled. He claimed that the Antikythera Mechanism was " . . . one of the greatest mechanical inventions of all time."

# STRANGE BUT TRUE STORIES

## THE STRANGE CASE OF THE SILENT TWINS

Lots of people envy twins their closeness. But sometimes there may be such a thing as *too much* closeness.

Jennifer and June Gibbons were twin girls born on April 11, 1963, in the West Indies. Their father was a technician in the British Royal Air Force. Soon after the girls were born, the Gibbons family was transferred to Wales.

From childhood, the twins seemed unusually close. They were inseparable. And they seemed determined to live in the world on *their* terms.

The twins chose not to speak to anyone except each other. And they used only a strange kind of language they'd made up for themselves. No one else could understand it.

If they had to communicate with

anyone else, they wrote notes—or simply grunted. Their mother and their teachers believed the twins were just very shy.

The twins' ties to each other grew even stronger. When the girls reached their teens, they locked themselves in their bedroom. They refused to take their meals with the rest of the family. Their mother had to deliver food to them on trays. And she slipped their mail to them under the bedroom door.

But things were not always good even when they were alone together. Family members often heard the girls talking and laughing. But just as often they heard the twins shouting and fighting.

At 13, the twins were sent to a psychotherapy center for treatment. But the therapy did no good. No one could break the wall of silence the twins had built around themselves.

Finally, a teacher suggested that the twins be separated and sent to different boarding schools. This was a disaster.

Each girl became entirely withdrawn and spoke to no one.

So they were reunited. Now they began to fill diaries with millions of words. They also wrote poetry, stories, and even novels. They weren't able to get their writing published by ordinary methods. Instead, they paid a vanity press to publish a novel that June wrote.

It was about this time that they also experimented with drugs. Then they started stealing small objects and setting fires in empty buildings. Finally, they were sent to Broadmoor, a high-security hospital for the criminally insane.

"Nobody suffers the way I do," June wrote in her diary. "This sister of mine, a dark shadow robbing me of sunlight, is my one and only torment."

Jennifer wrote, "I can read her mind, I know all about her moods. She's knowing, cunning, sly."

The twins were held in Broadmoor for 14 years. During that time, they became convinced that one of them would have to die so the other could live. And they agreed that the one who lived must begin to speak and lead a normal life.

After many lengthy discussions, Jennifer agreed to be the sacrifice.

In 1993, the twins were released from the hospital. Within hours, Jennifer was rushed to the hospital, where she died of a heart inflammation. What happened to her? Did she simply *will* herself to die? There were no drugs or poisons in her system. To this day, her death remains a mystery.

June returned home to live with her family. By all accounts, she is leading a normal life to this day.

# STRANGE BUT TRUE STORIES

## THE BELL WITCH

In 1804, John Bell moved his wife and children from North Carolina to Adams, Tennessee. There they settled on a large piece of property and built their farm.

The trouble began with John Bell's sickly neighbor, Kate Batts. She accused John of cheating her husband in a business deal. Even as she lay dying, she angrily vowed that she would get even with John from beyond the grave!

One day in 1817, John was walking in his field when he saw a strange animal. He shot at it, but when the smoke cleared, the animal had disappeared. John thought nothing more about the incident.

That night, however, strange noises sounded throughout the Bell house. Something knocked on doors and windows. The Bells heard odd noises. They heard wings flapping and the sounds of animals scratching and fighting. Family members looked everywhere, but none of them could find what was making the noises.

Night after night, the noises continued. Added to that, something was pulling sheets off the beds! Now the family was having a hard time getting any rest.

The Bells came to believe they had a poltergeist—a mischievous spirit—in their home.

John Bell didn't want his friends and neighbors to know what was happening in his house. He was afraid of what they might think. But finally, in a moment of desperation, he did tell a friend—James Johnson. Mr. Johnson and his wife asked if they could spend a night at the Bell house. They wanted to see the ghostly tricks for themselves. John Bell agreed.

Sure enough, the mischievous spirit played the same kinds of tricks on the Johnsons. Then Mr. Johnson came up with an idea. He asked the Bells if he could gather a small group of people to help him figure out what was happening. The Bells agreed, and every day a group gathered to pray and study the problem.

During this time, the spirit developed a voice. This was bad news—because the thing wouldn't stop talking. The spirit even identified herself as a female—who hated John Bell!

"The Bell Witch," as people began to call the spirit, played even more pranks. She would take sugar from the sugar bowl. She spilled the milk. She slapped and pinched the children—and then laughed at the pain she'd caused.

Word of the Bell Witch began to spread. General Andrew Jackson, who would eventually become President of the United States, heard about her. Jackson decided he would visit the Bell farm and look into the matter himself.

The general and several of his men traveled to the farm in a covered wagon. As they neared the farmhouse, the wagon suddenly stopped. The horses tried to pull it forward, but it wouldn't budge. The men got out and pushed. But no matter what they tried, the wagon wouldn't move forward. Finally, in frustration, General Jackson cried out, "It must be that witch!"

At exactly that moment, the wagon wheels began to roll forward.

That night Andrew Jackson, like everyone else, got a taste of the Bell Witch's pranks. The next day he left the farm. Later, he supposedly said that he'd rather face a whole army than deal with the Bell Witch!

In 1820, John Bell and his son were on their way to the hog barn. All of a sudden, one of John's shoes was ripped off his foot. Then the other shoe was torn off. The son helped John put his shoes back on. But after they walked a few more yards, an invisible hand slapped John across the face. The poor man was knocked off his feet!

Then the air filled with wild laughter, and John's eyes filled with tears. "Son," he said, "this horrible thing is killing me by slow torture. I don't think I have much longer to live."

Before long, John Bell was bedridden. Then one day, his sons found him lying unconscious on the barn floor.

The doctor came to him at once. He discovered that the medicine he'd prescribed for John had disappeared. In its place, there was a small brown bottle filled with a strange liquid. The liquid turned out to be poison.

The Bell Witch took credit for that, too. "He will never get up again," she screeched.

The next day, John Bell died. At his funeral, the Bell Witch reportedly interrupted the services by singing loud rowdy songs.

After John Bell's death, the Bell Witch's visits became fewer and fewer. Some people, however, believe that her spirit haunts the property to this day.

These days, a Tennessee Historical Marker near the site tells the story of the Bell Witch. It is the *only* historical marker in Tennessee to commemorate an unexplained paranormal event.

# STRANGE
## BUT TRUE STORIES

## THE BODY FARM

Do you wonder how investigators get so much information from a crime scene? How can they tell how long a victim has been dead? Or if the victim was moved after being murdered?

In 1971, Dr. Bill Bass was teaching at the University of Tennessee at Knoxville. An anthropologist, he studied the remains of ancient people.

Because of his special skills, he was often asked to help the police. When they found a dead body, they wanted to know when the victim had died. But the ancient people Dr. Bass studied had been dead for hundreds of years. The fresh bodies the police showed him were in various stages of decay. He didn't know much about the rate of decomposition. And he soon found that no one else knew, either.

Dr. Bass likes to tell a story about his

own ignorance. He was asked to tell how old a well-preserved corpse was. The victim had a gunshot wound to the head, and there was still flesh on his bones. Bass figured that the man had been killed a year ago. It turned out that the body was that of a Civil War soldier! He'd been well-preserved in a sealed lead coffin.

Bass can laugh now about his mistake. "I only missed it by 113 years! It made me realize how totally clueless we were about what happens in the hours after death. The only way to find out, I realized, was to watch a body rot."

The university gave him three acres of land and a few corpses of homeless men. Some bodies were left to decay on the ground. Some were put in the trunks of old cars or in underground vaults. Others were put in body bags. Then Dr. Bass and his graduate students went to work. They observed, they measured, and they wrote about what they were seeing.

Today, thanks to their efforts, medical

examiners know a lot more about what happens after death. They know which insects are attracted to dead bodies. They know that a body locked in a car decays faster than a body buried in the ground. They know that the soil underneath a body tells a story—even if the body has been removed from the crime scene.

Medical examiners, police officers, FBI agents, and doctors have all benefited from the Body Farm. Because of Dr. Bass's discoveries, crimes have been solved and murderers have been imprisoned. The police have also learned more about evaluating evidence.

You may have heard that *dead men tell no tales*. Thanks to Dr. Bass and his students, we know that the dead *do* talk! And the stories they tell may give would-be murderers second thoughts about committing a crime!

# STRANGE BUT TRUE STORIES

## THE MOTHMAN MYSTERY

From November 1966 to November 1967, the town of Point Pleasant, West Virginia, was a very bad place to visit. That was the year that a mysterious and frightening creature—nicknamed Mothman—terrorized local residents.

On November 12, 1966, five cemetery workers were preparing a grave when they saw something weird. They said it "looked like a brown human being flying out of the trees." They watched it for nearly a minute.

Two days later, another resident saw something hovering over a field near his house. The man's dog, Bandit, ran into the field. Bandit was never seen again.

The next night two couples were driving in a desolate area near Point Pleasant. Suddenly they spotted a figure standing by the side of the road. They later said that it was shaped like a very big man—maybe six or seven feet tall. But it had wings folded against its back and huge, red, glowing eyes!

The driver sped up until he was traveling more than 100 miles an hour. To his horror, the creature spread its wings and flew after the car! All four of the passengers noticed that the creature's wings didn't flap. Its wingspan was more than ten feet across, they added.

The press soon got hold of the story. A newspaper editor dubbed the creature "Mothman" after the popular Batman series on TV at that time.

On November 16, the Thomas family was expecting guests. When the guests arrived, their car disturbed something lying on the ground. "It rose up slowly," they said, "a big gray thing—bigger than a man—with terrible glowing red eyes."

When the guests ran from their car to the house, the figure shuffled along behind them. It climbed onto the porch and peered in through the window. But by the time they called the police, the creature disappeared into the darkness.

Two firemen saw the creature on November 18, and on November 21, Mothman was sighted sitting on a roof. On November 27, it was spotted on a golf course. And five pilots saw it flying about 70 miles an hour on December 4. They also said its wings weren't moving.

The number of Mothman sightings stayed high until November 1967. After that the sightings became fewer and fewer. It is believed that the last sighting was in September 1968.

But was "The Year of Mothman" an isolated event? Some people believe that Mothman is not a single creature. They point out that it's been spotted elsewhere in the world.

In 1946, winged, human-like creatures were spotted in Sweden. In 1963, four teenagers saw a Mothman-like creature in England. And in Cornwall, England, in 1976, three children saw a winged man who hissed at them. They described the huge man as having glowing red eyes.

Oddly enough, there have been reports throughout history of Mothman-like creatures. Many Nataive American tribes have legends that tell of giant bird-like creatures with glowing red eyes. In all cases, the creatures caused great fear among the humans who saw them.

It seems clear that the people of Point Pleasant saw *something*! There were too many believable witnesses to discount the story. Perhaps it was just a huge bird, such as a sand crane, as some critics have suggested. Or is Mothman a supernatural creature? An alien being? Or a freak of nature we've not yet identified? To this day, it's an unsolved mystery.

## THE SHADOW WOLVES

The Shadow Wolves moved across the rocky landscape, each with a tight feeling in the pit of his stomach. This time they weren't tracking drug smugglers or illegals. They were searching for a toddler—a little boy who'd wandered into the desert with his dog.

The child's family was frantic with worry. Search aircraft and trackers with dogs were called in right away. But no one had been able to find the child.

After everyone else had tried and failed, the three Shadow Wolves went to work. But time was running out. They knew the Arizona desert was a scary and dangerous place for a lost child.

Determined to find the boy in time, the Shadow Wolves worked through the night. And they *did* find him! It's a story they like to remember—a gripping tale with a very happy ending to it.

The Shadow Wolves are an elite U.S. Customs Service tracking patrol. Formed in 1972, the first patrol was made up of seven men of the Tohono O'odham Indian tribe. Today, the Shadow Wolves come from many tribes, including Navaho, Sioux, Lakota, Pima, Tohono O'odham, and more.

How do the Shadow Wolves succeed when dogs and planes fail? The 20 men and two women who make up the current patrol use ancient tracking methods. They call it "cutting for sign." "Cutting" is meticulous searching. "Sign" is physical evidence—such things as footprints, broken twigs, bits of thread, and tire tracks.

Their headquarters is on the Tohono O'odham reservation in southwestern Arizona. The reservation stretches to the border between the United States and Mexico.

Every year thousands of people come

into the United States illegally from Mexico. Some are drug smugglers. Others are illegal immigrants. And recently, a new threat has arisen: terrorists!

The Shadow Wolves use some modern technology, such as night vision goggles and radios for communication. But as yet there are no tools that can electronically or mechanically spot the tracks of someone crossing rough ground. "We have the new technology," says one Shadow Wolf. "But that doesn't mean that the new is better than the old."

When it comes to tracking, the ancient skills of the Native Americans are still the most effective.

The fame of the Shadow Wolves has spread around the world. As a result, the elite team has been invited to Europe and Asia. The Shadow Wolves teach tracking to law enforcement officers in various countries there. Some smugglers in those countries deal with extremely dangerous substances. Nuclear, chemical, and biological weapons are just a few examples.

The Shadow Wolves live by a saying that tells a lot about who they are and what they do:

> *In brightest day,*
> *in darkest night,*
> *no evil shall escape my sight,*
> *for I am a Shadow Wolf.*

# STRANGE
BUT TRUE STORIES

## THE DARK HISTORY
## OF NURSERY RHYMES

Most people are familiar with *Ring Around the Rosy* and *London Bridge Is Falling Down*. Little children have played these charming nursery rhyme games for generations.

But these rhymes weren't always "fun and games." In fact, both of them have a dark and frightening history.

In 1665, the bubonic plague—also called The Black Death—arrived in London. This horrifying disease was brought to the city by rats that had stowed away on ships. No one had any idea how to stop the infection from spreading. The words to the innocent-sounding nursery rhyme tell the story of this terrible time.

*Ring around the rosy:* Victims of the plague broke out with a rosy red rash in the shape of a ring.

*A pocketful of posies:* At that time, some people believed that the plague was spread by bad odors. So they carried sweet-smelling flowers and herbs in their pockets to protect themselves.

*Ashes, Ashes:* So many people died that the bodies had to be burned in big, smoky "plague pits."

*We all fall down:* The last word, which is now left out of the rhyme, is *dead*. About a third of London's population died during that awful outbreak.

In 1666, a raging fire broke out that destroyed much of London. But it also killed many of the rats. Some people believe that the fire actually stopped the spread of the disease.

* * *

*London Bridge Is Falling Down* is another favorite nursery rhyme game you probably played as a child. Very few people know that this rhyme also refers to a grim reality from the past.

In ancient times, people's beliefs were

based on superstition rather than science. Many believed that there was just one sure way to keep a bridge standing. That was to offer a human sacrifice by building a living person into the structure.

The sacrifice was often a child or an innocent young woman—the *My Fair Lady* of the rhyme. The idea was that the person walled up in the bridge's foundation would become a guardian spirit. That's what is meant by *Set a watch to watch all night*, another line in the rhyme.

People in countries around the world shared this grisly superstition. Even today, when ancient bridges are torn down, skeletons are sometimes found in the foundations. According to one legend, the stones of the real London Bridge were once spattered with the blood of little children!

# STRANGE BUT TRUE STORIES

## THE MYSTERY OF THE LOST ROANOKE COLONY

How could 117 people simply vanish off the face of the earth? This is the mystery that still surrounds Roanoke Colony, the first English settlement established in America.

The year they disappeared was 1587. And the place was Roanoke Island off the coast of North Carolina.

In 1584, Sir Walter Raleigh finally got his way. He'd convinced the Queen of England to let him establish a colony on Roanoke Island.

In 1585, Raleigh sent a party of 100 men to the island. Unfortunately, they had problems from the beginning. They arrived too late to begin planting, and their supplies ran low. Worse yet, the man in charge had made enemies of the local Indians by treating them very badly.

When Raleigh visited in 1586, the settlers had had enough. They insisted on returning to England. As luck would have it, a supply ship arrived just a week after they left. The captain was dismayed to find the island deserted. He left 15 of his men behind and returned to England for reinforcements.

In 1587, Raleigh sent a second group of 117 men, women, and children to Roanoke Island. He put John White in charge. White's daughter, Eleanor Dare, and her husband were among the settlers.

Shortly after they arrived at the island, Eleanor Dare gave birth to a baby girl. Virginia Dare was the first white child born in America.

What had happened to the 15 men who were left to hold down the fort? The new party of settlers soon learned that angry Indians had killed them! That made the settlers uneasy about remaining on the island, but they had no choice.

Before long John White was forced to

return to England for more supplies. He sailed away with a heavy heart, worried about his family—and with good reason! He never saw them again.

Because of unforeseen circumstances, White was unable to go back to Roanoke for three years. When he did return, he found that the colonists had vanished! The settlement was deserted. He did find two puzzling clues. On a tall wooden post someone had carved the word "CROATOAN." And on a nearby tree, White found the letters "CRO" carved into the trunk.

White hoped he would find the settlers on the island of Croatoan, which was south of Roanoke Island. This was the home of the Croatoan Indians.

But before he could search for the settlers, a hurricane damaged his ships. Forced back to England, he was unable to raise the money to return to America. John White died without ever learning about what happened to his family.

So, do historians know what *did* happen to the 117 colonists? Did they really vanish into thin air?

More than 120 years later, in 1709, an English explorer named John Lawson visited Roanoke Island. He also spent some time with the Indians on Croatoan Island. They told him that several of their ancestors had been white people. He observed that some of these Indians had light hair and gray eyes.

In 1888, a man named Hamilton MacMillan wrote about the Pembroke Indians. According to MacMillan, the Pembrokes spoke pure English and had the last names of many of the lost colonists. He added that they also had fair hair and light-colored eyes.

Today, many historians believe that the colony split into two groups after White left. The largest group traveled to Chesapeake Bay. There they settled near the friendly Chesapeake Indians on the south side of the Bay. In time, however, hostile Indians attacked and murdered most of them.

What happened to the second group that remained on Roanoke? They may have fled to the island of Croatoan. Did they willingly remain there and make friends with Indians? Did Virginia Dare grow up as a member of an Indian tribe?

No clues have been found to tell us what happened. To this day their fate remains a mystery.

# STRANGE
## BUT TRUE STORIES

## BURKE AND HARE—
## THE BODY SNATCHERS

In the 1800s, doctors needed bodies to study and use as teaching tools. But trying to find a supply of fresh corpses was difficult. Most grieving relatives didn't want their loved ones' bodies to be used in that way.

In desperation, some doctors resorted to an illegal way of getting what they needed: body snatching. They paid ruthless men to dig up bodies that had recently been buried. The fresher the corpse, the more money the body snatchers were paid. The doctors never asked where the bodies came from, and the body snatchers never told. Why? The punishment for the crime of body snatching was hanging!

In 1818, two men named William Burke and William Hare moved from

Ireland to Scotland. They came to work on the Union Canal. The two men met when Burke became a tenant in a boarding house that Hare helped manage.

One night an elderly man who lived at the boarding house died. He owed Hare back rent. So Burke and Hare decided to sell his body to Dr. Robert Knox. Dr. Knox taught at a medical school in the city of Edinburgh.

It was the beginning of a profitable business relationship.

Their next victim was another tenant who was dying of the plague. Hare was nervous. If the authorities knew about the sick man, they might close down the boarding house. And that would put him out of business. So Burke and Hare decided to help the dying man along. After Burke smothered the sick man, they sold his body to Dr. Knox.

At this point, Burke and Hare had run out of easy-to-find bodies. So they took matters into their own hands. First, they lured a poor woman into the boarding house. Then Burke smothered her. He'd figured out that smothering a person left no marks on the body.

Thus began their killing spree, which lasted about nine months. During that time, Burke and Hare murdered 16 people. They sold the bodies to their only customer, Dr. Knox.

As time went by, the body snatchers became more and more reckless. In the end, they took too many chances. Other tenants in the boarding house were becoming suspicious of Hare.

One night the tenants came home early and found a fresh body. When they reported it to the police, Burke and Hare were quickly arrested.

Burke was found guilty of murder and hanged. Hare was kicked out of Scotland. And Dr. Knox was run out of Edinburgh by an angry mob.

This grisly case had one good result. A law was soon passed that helped doctors obtain bodies for teaching and studying. This was the Anatomy Act of 1832. It allowed doctors access to unclaimed cadavers from hospitals, workhouses, and prisons.

As for Burke and Hare, in Scotland they are still remembered in a children's nursery rhyme:

*Up the close and down the stair,*
*In the house with Burke and Hare.*
*Burke's the butcher, Hare's the thief,*
*Knox, the boy who buys the beef.*

# STRANGE BUT TRUE STORIES

## ROBERT, THE EVIL DOLL

In 1900, Robert Eugene Otto was born in Key West, Florida. Gene, as he came to be called, was the youngest of the family's three boys.

The Ottos were a well-to-do family. But, unfortunately, money did not make them kind. By many accounts, they were often cruel to their servants. One of the servants who was very badly treated was a young girl. It happened that she knew a few things about voodoo. To get even, she made a special doll for young Gene. Some say that she sewed a curse in it.

Gene gave the doll his own first name, Robert, and took it everywhere with him. Robert was about three feet tall and made of straw. Reportedly, the doll had been made to look just like the boy. He even wore clothes like Gene's.

It soon became clear that Robert was

not an ordinary doll. Mr. and Mrs. Otto sometimes heard Gene talking to Robert. Of course it's not unusual for a child to talk to a toy. But someone—or some *thing*—always answered in a completely different voice. Who was talking? Was it Gene or was it Robert?

Strange things began to happen in the Otto house. Pictures fell off the walls and broke. Doors locked themselves. But no matter what happened, Gene always said, "Robert did it."

Perhaps Gene was right. Other people claimed to have heard the doll giggle. Still others said they had seen it running up the stairs. People walking by the house sometimes saw the doll watching them from the turret-room window!

Gene was a talented artist. In time, he grew up and went away to school. For several years he lived in Europe, where he studied and painted. It was in Paris that he met his wife, Anne.

Then Gene's parents died, and he

inherited the house. When Gene and Anne moved in, the young husband found Robert in the attic. Gene's fixation on the evil doll began all over again.

Anne hated Robert—and she especially hated her husband's fascination with the doll. Finally, to make Anne happy, Gene put Robert in the tower room. Still, Anne claimed she could hear someone laughing and running around in that room. But when she went upstairs to see what it was, she found only Robert.

Gene and Anne died in the 1970s. Robert was taken to the Key West Martello Museum, where he's on display today. But beware! Visitors report that their cameras malfunction when they try to photograph Robert.

Some also report hearing someone—or some *thing*—tapping on the glass of Robert's display case. When they turn to look, they see the doll's hand on the glass. Is Robert still scaring people?

# STRANGE BUT TRUE STORIES

## WHO WAS THE REAL SHERLOCK HOLMES?

All fans of detective stories are familiar with the ingenious private detective, Sherlock Holmes. British writer Sir Arthur Conan Doyle created Holmes and his sidekick, Dr. Watson, in the late 1800s.

Sherlock Holmes could always solve mysteries that baffled the police and everyone else. He was famous for his ability to figure out where a person had come from, what he or she did for a living, what his or her problem was, and much more—just by observation.

Holmes' powers of deduction were amazing. But how realistic were they? Could a real person be that clever?

Yes, indeed! Sherlock Holmes was based on a real person, a man Conan Doyle knew—Dr. Joseph Bell.

In 1877, Conan Doyle enrolled at the

University of Edinburgh in Scotland. The young man was studying to be a doctor, and Dr. Bell was one of his professors.

In Dr. Bell's time, doctors had to pay close attention to every detail about their patients. They didn't have the modern technology that helps today's doctors make a diagnosis. The little things they observed were the clues that helped them find the cause of an illness.

Dr. Bell told his students to carefully observe a new patient. The students' task was to figure out what was wrong with the man. Dr. Bell told them not to touch the patient—but to use only their eyes, ears, and brains. After looking the patient over, one student decided that the man was suffering from hip-joint disease.

Dr. Bell snorted with laughter. "Hip-nothing!" he snapped. "The man's limp is not from his hip. It's from his foot, or rather from his feet." Dr. Bell pointed out the slits cut in the man's shoes. They'd been put there to relieve the pressure of corns!

Doyle's first story about Sherlock Holmes was published in a British magazine. It was a huge success, and the author soon became world famous. He credited Dr. Bell as the model he'd used for the popular detective. Dr. Bell was very pleased to have been Conan Doyle's inspiration.

But what about Dr. Watson, the narrator of the Sherlock Holmes stories? Who did Conan Doyle use as the model for Holmes's sidekick?

He patterned the doctor after *himself*!

# STRANGE BUT TRUE STORIES

## BOB LAZAR, THE UFO GUY

Just mention the words "Area 51" and many people think of UFOs. Area 51 is a top-secret military base in the Nevada desert. It's a very closely guarded place. Anyone who strays too near it may be arrested or, some say—shot!

Area 51 is rumored to be the home of recovered alien aircraft. People who believe that UFOs have crashed on Earth think that scientists there are studying flying saucers. That might explain the strange-looking aircraft some people say they've seen flying over the area at night.

But surely all this is nothing more than guesswork. Or is it?

In 1989, a man named Bob Lazar came forward to make an amazing claim. He said he'd worked on a special project at Area 51—a project that involved no less than nine recovered flying saucers!

"This stuff came from somewhere else," Lazar told TV investigative reporter George Knapp. "I know it's hard to believe, but it's there—I saw it."

What exactly did Lazar see?

He says that he actually saw an alien spacecraft fly. He also says he looked inside and saw very small chairs. "Why would people of normal size need such small furniture?" he asks.

Lazar went on to tell Knapp that the flying saucers were fueled by something called Element 115. But in 1989, Element 115 did not exist. It wasn't until 2004 that a team of scientists created a small amount of Element 115 in a lab!

Knapp and his staff tried to check Lazar's credentials—but that was hard to do. Lazar told them where he went to college and what degrees he had earned. But when those colleagues were contacted, none of them had ever heard of him.

Lazar mentioned other places he'd worked, including the Los Alamos

National Labs. Officials at Los Alamos claimed they had no record of Lazar's employment. Lazar's name, however, was listed along with other scientists in a 1982 edition of the lab's phone book.

Today, Bob Lazar doesn't like to talk about UFOs. He lives in New Mexico now, where he's working on engines fueled by hydrogen.

Lazar's critics claim he's a fraud. They say he isn't even a real scientist. But it's a fact that Lazar has built jet engines and hydrogen systems, as well as particle accelerators.

So is Bob Lazar a fraud? Or does the government not want anyone to know that he worked on alien spacecraft at Area 51? You decide.

# STRANGE BUT TRUE STORIES

## MIXED MESSAGES

People who say they're "seeing red" mean that they're very angry.

Colorful figures of speech are common. We "see red" when we're mad and "feel blue" when we're sad. But scientists estimate that perhaps one of every 2,000 people actually do taste, smell, feel, or hear color!

Why do some people experience such an unusual sensory mix-up? They have a rare neurological condition. It's called *synesthesia*. For them, two or more of their five senses—taste, smell, touch, hearing, and sight—are tangled together.

"Experiencing" a color in response to seeing an object is the most common combination of "mixed signals." But there are many more.

Can you imagine what it would be like to see or touch a sound? To taste or smell a vision? What would it be like to hear a horn honk every time you bit into an apple? Or to see your world turn orange when you hear the sound of a bird singing? Or to smell the scent of skunk every time you saw the family pet!

Here are some stories from a few people who have this fascinating condition.

One woman describes how music affects her. "I physically *feel* sound," she says. "To me, the strum of a guitar feels like someone blowing on my ankles. And piano music presses on my chest over my heart. New Orleans jazz hits me all over—like heavy, sharp raindrops."

Another woman feels pain in color. "The pain from my injured shin throbbed in orange and yellow," she reported.

One man tastes in Technicolor. "To me," he says, "the taste of beef is blue. Fish is green. Every time I eat, I experience a rainbow of colors."

Some perceive written numbers, letters, and words in color. One woman said, "I always see the letter J as light green and the number 8 as orange."

Sometimes the sensations can be overwhelming. One woman shared this experience:

"I asked an ice cream vendor about the 'flavor of the day.' When she said 'tutti frutti,' I suddenly saw hot coals bursting from her mouth! Then smoke and fog swirled around us. I had to leave without having any ice cream," she finished sadly.

There was a time when people with this condition were thought to be hallucinating or suffering from delusions. Today, however, scientists know this is not the case. In fact, synesthesia may prove to be beneficial to humankind. Studying what causes this condition may help scientists better understand how the brain is organized.

## THE MUTTER MUSEUM—
## OH, GROSS!

In 1849, a strange museum was created at the College of Physicians in Philadelphia. Its purpose was to house specimens of human anatomy that might otherwise be lost to science.

In 1856, Dr. Thomas Dent Mutter wrote to the museum. He said that he was donating his collection of specimens. Along with his collection, Dr. Mutter gave a gift of money. The funds were to pay the salaries of a museum curator and a lecturer. There was also enough money to maintain and enlarge the museum. Mutter specified that plans should be drawn up to house the museum in a new fireproof building.

In 1863, the museum moved into its new quarters. As the years went by, many more collections of specimens were added.

At first, only members of the medical profession used the museum. Today, it's open to the general public. But this isn't an exhibition for the faint of heart—or the weak of stomach. This is an assembly of body parts or casts of body parts—some of the strangest body parts ever seen.

One of the oddest attractions is the famous Soap Woman. Unearthed in Philadelphia, this is the body of an obese woman who died during the yellow fever epidemic of 1792–1793. After she died, she was buried in soil that contained certain chemicals. Those chemicals turned the woman's body fat into soap!

The skeleton of a man from Kentucky who stood seven feet, six inches tall is on display as well. Right next to him is the skeleton of a tiny midget.

Another exhibit features the brain of John Wilson, a murderer who was hanged in Pennsylvania. It is just one of many brains on display.

Another odd attraction is the gallery of human horns. Did you know that human beings can grow horns? Apparently they can—and not only on their heads, but also on the backs of their hands!

There's a fascinating array of objects that doctors had to remove from people who swallowed them. These items include bones, coins, shells, and even dentures.

Some medical instruments are also exhibited at the Mutter. This gallery includes the wooden stethoscope made by the doctor who invented it in 1816. It also displays an iron lung from the terrible days when polio was a dreaded and mysterious disease.

The Mutter Museum contains about 20,000 amazing displays. If you like your museum displays *unusual*—this might be just the place for you.

But just remember, as you walk through the museum's galleries, this is *not* the place to shout, "Oh, gross!"

# STRANGE BUT TRUE STORIES

## DO WE GET WHAT WE DESERVE?

Is it possible for anyone to get away with murder?

There are plenty of stories about people who do. But do these criminals usually end up being punished in some other way?

This is the story of the Donner Party—a terrible American tragedy—and of a man who seemed to go unpunished. Or did he?

In 1846, a wagon train set out on the journey from Missouri to California. The pioneers making the trip included 87 men, women, and children. Only 46 of these people reached California alive.

The journey began well enough. The wagon train followed the Oregon trail until they reached Fort Bridger. There they met a man named Lansford Hastings. He told them about a shorter route to

California. He claimed that it would save them a lot of time.

The leaders of the Donner Party decided to take Hastings' advice. It was a terrible and deadly mistake. Winter had already hit when the Donner Party reached the Sierra Nevada Mountains. They continued up the slopes, but eventually the snow blocked their path going forward—and also their way back! They were stuck in a place that later became known as Donner Lake.

The weary pioneers were desperately short of food. They killed and ate their animals one by one. Their attempts at hunting and fishing were largely unsuccessful. Soon the weakest members of the party were dying of starvation.

Some members of the party decided to walk out of the mountains. Their aim was to reach California and get help. They, too, were short of food and very weak. Some of them, however, did make it to California. One rescue party after another was sent to save the survivors. Finally, a rescue party managed to reach Donner Lake. The rescuers were astonished to learn how the survivors had stayed alive. Driven by desperation, they'd resorted to cannibalism. They had eaten the flesh of the dead!

Only one man—Lewis Keseberg—was actually accused of murder. But was he guilty? And if so, was he punished?

Keseberg began making enemies early in the journey. Along the trail, he was accused of stealing a buffalo robe from an Indian burial scaffold. This charge was never proved. But some people in the wagon train believed that he did it.

A charge that *could* be proved was that Keseberg was very abusive. He was a man with a vicious temper—and he often beat his young wife. Finally, another member of the party threatened Keseberg if he didn't stop.

Keseberg was also accused of banishing an elderly man from the wagon train. The old man had been traveling with the Keseberg family, and perhaps he was unable to keep up. Then other members of the party realized the old man was missing. They searched for him, but they never found him. Some people believed that Keseberg had killed the old man. Others thought he'd abandoned the old fellow in the wilderness.

Then came the full force of winter at Donner Lake. As each new rescue party reached the lake, the rescuers could take out only so many people at a time. Some had to stay behind.

When the third rescue party departed from the lake, Keseberg and a handful of others were left behind. When the fourth rescue party arrived, only Keseberg was found alive!

Members of the fourth party made a shocking claim. They said that Keseberg had actually murdered one or more people in order to eat them! But there was no proof. Lewis Keseberg was never formally arrested and charged with murder.

But after Keseberg was rescued, the rumors started to circulate. What had the last rescue party found in and near Keseberg's cabin? Some witnesses said that Keseberg had been cooking part of a human being in a big pot! They claimed he admitted that he preferred to eat human flesh. Several said he looked and acted like a wild man.

Later, Keseberg sued a member of the rescue party for spreading scandalous stories. He won his case—but he was awarded only one dollar in damages. The judge didn't think his reputation was worth more than that!

Keseberg's reputation as a monster followed him wherever he went. In 1847, he was hired to work on a Sacramento riverboat. He was soon replaced, however. According to one source, he made the passengers nervous. They were afraid that if they ran out of food, the monster Keseberg might kill and eat them!

From then on, he had nothing but bad luck. In 1851, Keseberg bought a hotel—but it was soon destroyed by fire. Another business he purchased was destroyed by flood. Twice he was arrested and tried for assault. His wife and most of their eleven children died before he did.

At the end of his life, Keseberg was poverty-stricken. There were no family members to care for him, and he had no friends. In 1895, he died in Sacramento. He was buried in an unknown spot. His grave was unmarked.

By contrast, his descendants placed a proper marker on the graves of his wife and her children.

Perhaps there's some truth in the old saying: *What goes around comes around.* It would seem that the great harm Lewis Keseberg caused others had indeed come back to haunt him.